Microwave Magic
Gifts from the Kitchen

Grolier Limited
TORONTO

Contributors to this series:

Recipes and Technical Assistance:
École de cuisine Bachand-Bissonnette
Cooking consultants:
Denis Bissonette
Michèle Émond
Dietician:
Christiane Barbeau
Photos:
Laramée Morel Communications
Audio-Visuelles
Design:
Claudette Taillefer
Assistants:
Julie Deslauriers
Philippe O'Connor
Joan Pothier
Accessories:
Andrée Cournoyer
Writing:
Communications La Griffe Inc.
Text Consultants:
Cap et bc inc.
Advisors:
Roger Aubin
Joseph R. De Varennes
Gaston Lavoie
Kenneth H. Pearson

Assembly:
Carole Garon
Vital Lapalme
Jean-Pierre Larose
Carl Simmons
Gus Soriano
Marc Vallières
Production Managers:
Gilles Chamberland
Ernest Homewood
Production Assistants:
Martine Gingras
Catherine Gordon
Kathy Kishimoto
Peter Thomlison
Art Director:
Bernard Lamy
Editors:
Laurielle Ilacqua
Susan Marshall
Margaret Oliver
Robin Rivers
Lois Rock
Jocelyn Smyth
Donna Thomson
Dolores Williams
Development:
Le Groupe Polygone Éditeurs Inc.

The series editors have taken every care to ensure that the information given is accurate. However, no cookbook can guarantee the user successful results. The editors cannot accept any responsibility for the results obtained by following the recipes and recommendations given.

We wish to thank the following firms, PIER I IMPORTS and LE CACHE POT, for their contribution to the illustration of this set.

Canadian Cataloguing in Publication Data

Main entry under title:

Gifts from the kitchen

(Microwave magic)
Includes index.
ISBN 0-7172-2596-8

1. Confectionary.   2. Baking.   3. Microwave cooking.   I. Series: Microwave magic (Toronto, Ont.)

TX832.C36 1989   641.8'6   C89-093483-5

Contents

Microwave Magic is a multi-volume set, with each volume devoted to a particular type of cooking. So, if you are looking for a chicken recipe, you simply go to one of the two volumes that deal with poultry. Each volume has its own index, and the final volume contains a general index to the complete set.

Microwave Magic puts over twelve hundred recipes at your fingertips. You will find it as useful as the microwave oven itself. Enjoy!

Note from the Editor

How to Use this Book

The books in this set have been designed to make your job as easy as possible. As a result, most of the recipes are set out in a standard way.

We suggest that you begin by consulting the information chart for the recipe you have chosen. You will find there all the information you need to decide if you are able to make it: preparation time, cost per serving, level of difficulty, number of calories per serving and other relevant details. Thus, if you have only 30 minutes in which to prepare the evening meal, you will quickly be able to tell which recipe is possible and suits your schedule.

The list of ingredients is always clearly separated from the main text. When space allows, the ingredients are shown together in a photograph so that you can make sure you have them all without rereading the list— another way of saving your valuable time. In addition, for the more complex recipes we have supplied photographs of the key stages involved either in preparation or serving.

All the dishes in this book have been cooked in a 700 watt microwave oven. If your oven has a different wattage, consult the conversion chart that appears on the following page for cooking times in different types of oven. We would like to emphasize that the cooking times given in the book are a minimum. If a dish does not seem to be cooked enough, you may return it to the oven for a few more minutes. Also, the cooking time can vary according to your ingredients: their water and fat content, thickness, shape and even where they come from. We have therefore left a blank space on each recipe page in which you can note the cooking time that suits you best. This will enable you to add a personal touch to the recipes that we suggest and to reproduce your best results every time.

Although we have put all the technical information together at the front of this book, we have inserted a number of boxed entries called **MICROTIPS** through-out to explain particular techniques. They are brief and simple, and will help you obtain successful results in your cooking.

With the very first recipe you try, you will discover just how simple microwave cooking can be and how often it depends on techniques you already use for cooking with a conventional oven. If cooking is a pleasure for you, as it is for us, it will be all the more so with a microwave oven. Now let's get on with the food.

The Editor

Key to the Symbols

For ease of reference, the following symbols have been used on the recipe information charts.

The pencil symbol is a reminder to write your cooking time in the space provided.

Level of Difficulty

Easy

Moderate

Complex

Cost per Serving

$ Inexpensive

$ $ Moderate

$ $ $ Expensive

Power Levels

All the recipes in this book have been tested in a 700 watt oven. As there are many microwave ovens on the market with different power levels, and as the names of these levels vary from one manufacturer to another, we have decided to give power levels as a percentage. To adapt the power levels given here, consult the chart opposite and the instruction manual for your oven.

Generally speaking, if you have a 500 watt or 600 watt oven you should increase cooking times by about 30% over those given, depending on the actual length of time required. The shorter the original cooking time, the greater the percentage by which it must be lengthened. The 30% figure is only an average. Consult the chart for detailed information on this topic.

Power Levels

HIGH: 100% - 90%	Vegetables (except boiled potatoes and carrots) Soup Sauce Fruits Browning ground beef Browning dish Popcorn
MEDIUM HIGH: 80% - 70%	Rapid defrosting of precooked dishes Muffins Some cakes Hot dogs
MEDIUM: 60% - 50%	Cooking tender meat Cakes Fish Seafood Eggs Reheating Boiled potatoes and carrots
MEDIUM LOW: 40%	Cooking less tender meat Simmering Melting chocolate
DEFROST: 30% **LOW: 30% - 20%**	Defrosting Simmering Cooking less tender meat
WARM: 10%	Keeping food warm Allowing yeast dough to rise

Cooking Time Conversion Chart

700 watts	600 watts*
5 s	11 s
15 s	20 s
30 s	40 s
45 s	1 min
1 min	1 min 20 s
2 min	2 min 40 s
3 min	4 min
4 min	5 min 20 s
5 min	6 min 40 s
6 min	8 min
7 min	9 min 20 s
8 min	10 min 40 s
9 min	12 min
10 min	13 min 30 s
20 min	26 min 40 s
30 min	40 min
40 min	53 min 40 s
50 min	66 min 40 s
1 h	1 h 20 min

* There is very little difference in cooking times between 500 watt ovens and 600 watt ovens.

Gifts from the Kitchen

"It is more blessed to give than to receive"—so goes the old adage that we all know so well. But the pleasure of giving can be doubled when your offering is the result of your efforts in the kitchen. A cheerful bow, a colorful container filled with dainty mouth-watering confections—a gift that is sure to please.

The Pleasure of Offering . . .

There is no need to spend a lot of money and time making containers for your offerings. Friends are easily pleased. A tin box, a cardboard box covered with colorful gift wrap, a glass jar decorated with a pretty piece of fabric, a perky bow and a fancy label—any of these will do the trick. Let your imagination run wild; that's part of the fun.

. . . Cakes and Dainties

The aroma of freshly baked cakes and cookies, still warm from the oven, cannot be equalled. This is probably one of the first pleasures in life experienced by young children. However, we don't bake simply to enjoy the delicious aromas!

Perhaps you have decided to spend a cold winter afternoon in your warm kitchen. Perhaps a special birthday dinner is coming up. Or, perhaps you would like to offer neighbors a token of appreciation at Christmas time. There is a special joy in doing some fancy baking: two-tone pinwheel cookies or rosewater cookies, spaceship cupcakes or miniature fantasy cakes. Can't you imagine the happy faces of your family and friends? You know these gifts from your kitchen will really be appreciated!

. . . Confections

The art of making candy and other fancy sweets is one that delights the self-indulgent among us as well as anyone with a sweet tooth. The different kinds of fudge, the thick smooth caramels, the chocolates that melt in the mouth—all these recipes that we have prepared for you are easy to make and require just a little care to achieve success. On pages 12 and 13 you will find instructions on how to cook with sugar as well as a chart showing the various stages of cooking sugar, which we are sure you will find helpful. You will find great satisfaction in presenting such offerings as our desert roses, orange wafers or tasty caramel crunch.

. . . Preserves

If you wish to give a gift that will last longer than a few days, why not try some delicious preserves? Luscious fruit or fresh, firm vegetables, preserved in sugar or vinegar, provide a delicious accompaniment to many dishes. Whether you choose our zucchini jam, marinated antipasto, apple chutney or cranberry preserve, you will please your friends by sharing nature's bounty with them.

The Art of Baking—Microwave Style

Adapting Recipes to the Microwave

In your first attempt at adapting a recipe for cakes or dainties to microwave cooking, try a "proven" recipe. It will be much easier for you to identify changes that are required if you are already familiar with the desired results. If you want to experiment with an untried recipe, choose one that you can appreciate and enjoy; a recipe that doesn't impress you much will not be improved just because it was cooked in the microwave oven.

Many traditional recipes can be converted for cooking in the microwave without changing the ingredients themselves. You must remember, however, that since liquids slow the cooking process and fats accelerate it, you must reduce the amount of liquid and fat in order to obtain a balance between the two. To obtain even cooking, you must give the dish a half-turn during the cooking and follow the directions given for a microwave recipe that is comparable to the one you are adapting. Remember never to use metal baking dishes in the microwave oven. Any other pan or dish, made of heat-resistant glass or plastic, may be used for cooking in the microwave. If you have a choice, circular molds and tube pans are preferable because they ensure more even cooking.

Using the microwave oven to do your baking does not automatically mean you must forget your old, favorite recipes. By following certain rules in converting recipes, measuring ingredients and using substitutes, you can easily adapt them to this new cooking method. Even in microwave cooking, baking remains an art in which precision is a guarantee of success.

Measuring Ingredients

Here are some rules concerning the measurement of ingredients. They are well-known rules but a quick reminder never hurts.

1. To measure liquids accurately use a transparent measuring cup, one with a lip and pouring spout. Place the cup on a flat surface and measure at eye level to be precise in determining the level of the liquid to be measured.

2. Coat the inside of the measuring cup with a light film of oil before measuring such ingredients as honey, molasses or syrup. The oil prevents the substance from sticking to the measuring cup and ensures greater accuracy in measuring.

3. The volume of dry ingredients can vary greatly, depending on how they are measured. For accurate results, we recommend that ingredients such as flour and baking powder be heaped in proper measuring cups and spoons and then levelled with a knife or spatula when being measured. Brown sugar, on the other hand, is always packed down for measuring.

Substituting Ingredients

Perhaps you would like to experiment with some of your recipes for baked goods to obtain a little variety. Or, maybe you find yourself short of a certain ingredient. You can always substitute one item for another of the same type but sometimes quantities must be adjusted. The following chart contains a short list of common ingredients and possible substitutes for them, including the quantities required for each.

Common Ingredients and Possible Substitutes

Ingredient	Quantity	Substitute Ingredient
Baking powder	5 mL (1 teaspoon)	1 mL (1/4 teaspoon) baking soda plus 3 mL (3/4 teaspoon) cream of tartar
Butter or margarine	250 mL (1 cup)	250 mL (1 cup) cooking oil plus 2 mL (1/2 teaspoon) salt
Chocolate, unsweetened	30 g (1 ounce)	30 mL (2 tablespoons) cocoa powder plus 30 mL (2 tablespoons) butter
Flour, all purpose	500 mL (2 cups)	400 mL (1-2/3 cups) whole wheat flour
Flour, cake and pastry	250 mL (1 cup)	225 mL (7/8 cup) sifted all purpose flour plus 7 mL (1-1/2 teaspoons) baking powder plus 2 mL (1/2 teaspoon) salt
Honey	250 mL (1 cup)	250 mL (1 cup) sugar plus 50 mL (1/4 cup) liquid
Lemon zest, grated	5 mL (1 teaspoon)	2 mL (1/2 teaspoon) lemon extract
Sugar, brown	250 mL (1 cup)	175 mL (3/4 cup) granulated sugar plus 50 mL (1/4 cup) molasses
Sugar, icing	425 mL (1-3/4 cups)	250 mL (1 cup) granulated sugar

Confectionery: Sugar and Its Properties

Most dictionaries agree on the definition of the word "confectionery": the art of producing candy and other fancy sweets made with sugar. Sugar, like chocolate, will always be associated with confections. Where did this product come from—so readily available today but almost impossible to come by a few centuries ago?

In the sixth century BC the expedition of Darius Ist, King of Persia, discovered "a reed that produced honey without the assistance of bees" in the valleys of India. The Persians were regarded as the experts on sugar cane for twelve centuries, until the Arab invasion in the seventh century AD. The Arabs then introduced the cultivation of sugar cane to the regions they conquered: Egypt, Rhodes, Cyprus, North Africa, Syria, southern Spain and Portugal. The Crusaders learned about this intriguing food and interest spread throughout Europe. The Portuguese, in turn, introduced sugar cane culture into their colonies in Africa and America between the sixteenth and seventeenth centuries. However, it was not until the nineteenth century that sugar from cane or beets was produced commercially.

It is the transformation of sugar by cooking that produces a large variety of candy. Sugar, boiled with or without liquid, evaporates and becomes more concentrated. The final temperature has a definite effect on the type of candy produced—from soft caramel to hard candies such as brittles. The less liquid a sugar mixture contains, the harder the final result when cooled. It is very difficult, however, to determine the correct temperature and thus the desired concentration of sugar syrup. We recommend the use of a candy thermometer when making candy; an exact reading on the thermometer along with an effective method for testing the cooking stage will ensure total success. In the opposite chart, you will find descriptions of twelve stages in cooking sugar, as well as the corresponding temperature, the appropriate testing method and the results you should look for in each case.

Stages for Cooking Sugar

Cooking Stage	Temperature	Method of testing	Result
Gloss	100°C (212°F)	Dip a slotted spoon into the syrup and shake gently.	The syrup clogs the holes in the spoon.
Small thread	102°C (215°F)	Place a thumb and index finger in cold water; allow a drop of syrup to fall between two fingers and separate the fingers quickly.	The syrup forms short thin threads that break easily.
Large thread	103°C (217°F)	Same method as for small thread stage.	The syrup stretches into longer threads before breaking.
Pearl	105°C (221°F)	Dip a slotted spoon into the syrup and remove.	The syrup that drips through the slots in the spoon forms small balls, round and close together, resembling pearls.
Thread	106°-113°C (223°-235°F)	Same method as for pearl stage.	The syrup forms a light thread.
Soft ball	112°-116°C (234°-241°F)	With a spoon, drop a bit of syrup into ice water and remove the ball that forms.	The ball keeps its shape in the water but flattens when pressed with the fingers; the ball is very sticky.
Firm ball	118°-121°C (244°-250°F)	Same method as for soft ball stage.	The ball is firm but malleable; the ball is sticky.
Hard ball	121°-130°C (250°-266°F)	Same method as for soft ball stage.	The ball keeps its shape and is firm when pressed with the fingers; the ball is sticky.
Small crack	132°-143°C (270°-289°F)	Same method as for soft ball stage.	The ball separates into hard but pliable elastic threads; the ball is not very sticky.
Large crack	149°-154°C (300°-309°F)	Same method as for soft ball stage.	The ball separates into hard, brittle threads that snap easily. The syrup turns a pale yellow.
Clear caramel	160°-170°C (320°-338°F)	Pour a little syrup into a white saucer.	The syrup is the color of honey.
Dark caramel	165°-177°C (329°-351°F)	Same method as for clear caramel stage.	The syrup is an amber color. Beyond this stage, the syrup becomes bitter.

The Art of Preserving

Enzymes and micro-organisms are the two main causes of food spoilage. Stopping or slowing down their action means we can enjoy the flavor of fresh fruit and vegetables long after they have been harvested.

Enzymes are proteins found in all living organisms, whether animal or vegetable. They play an important catalytic role in the various chemical reactions taking place in fruit and vegetables. These reactions continue to take place even after the fruit or vegetable has been harvested and have a distinct effect on flavor, color and texture.

Micro-organisms such as bacteria, molds or yeast are always present in the earth, air and water. Consequently, such micro-organisms are to be found in fresh food as well. Generally speaking, bacteria is the cause of most food poisoning. The gravity of such poisoning depends on the kind of bacteria and the toxins produced in the food. The only way to eliminate contamination by bacteria is to carefully follow the rules of hygiene and to take every precaution when processing fresh food for long-term storage. With the exception of Roquefort cheese, which is marbled with mold, and wine, which is produced by the action of yeast on the must of grapes, micro-organisms cause a

disagreeable taste in most foods and sometimes cause chemical reactions that are toxic. Therefore, the utmost care is required in the preparation of food to be preserved.

Cold as well as heat puts a stop to bacterial or enzyme action. Freezing is a very modern method of food preservation but heat is probably more efficient in stopping the action of the various agents that cause food spoilage. High temperatures destroy the bacteria and their toxins, thus stopping the catalytic action of the enzymes. However, sterilizing food is not enough in itself to prevent spoilage because contact with the air, in which micro-organisms are found, causes deterioration as well. It is therefore necessary to store foodstuffs in airtight containers; the heat applied in preserving food creates a vacuum, hermetically sealing containers. Sugar, vinegar or alcohol inhibits the growth of micro-organisms, but the method used for sealing is also a very important step in the preparation of all preserves. Glycerine paper or paraffin wax are often used to make effective seals.

Glycerine paper works well with fruit-based jams and jellies; the sugar content of these preserves is sufficient to stop all bacterial growth. You must make sure that the

containers you use are sterilized. Pour the hot jam or jelly into the containers and cover with a circle of glycerine paper cut to fit the neck of the jar. Run a finger over the surface of the paper to eliminate any air bubbles and cover immediately with jar lids or plastic wrap. Another approach is to wait until the preparation has completely cooled. If you try to proceed with this operation when the jam is still warm, you will seal a certain amount of moisture in, which will provide a medium for the growth of organisms; it is therefore essential that the mixture be completely cool.

Sealing with paraffin wax is ideal for chutneys and relishes because it prevents evaporation. Place a circle of glycerine paper over the preparation, remove any air bubbles and pour melted paraffin wax over the paper, making sure it seals itself to the neck of the jar. Allow the wax to harden and then place a lid on the jar.

Always store your preserves in a cool, dry, airy place or in the refrigerator. Your preserves will keep much better in there than in your traditional storage cupboard.

We suggest you consult the above chart for guidance as to what preserving agent should be used with different fruits and vegetables.

Preserving Agents for Various Fruits and Vegetables

Food	Salt	Sugar	Vinegar	Alcohol
Fruit:				
Apricots		X	X	X
Apples		X		
Blueberries		X		
Cherries		X	X	X
Currants		X		
Figs		X		
Grapefruit		X		
Grapes		X		
Lemons	X	X		
Limes	X	X		
Mandarins		X		
Melons		X	X	
Nectarines		X	X	X
Oranges		X		X
Peaches		X	X	X
Pears		X	X	X
Pineapple		X		
Plums		X	X	X
Raspberries		X		
Rhubarb		X		
Strawberries		X		
Vegetables:				
Beets		X	X	
Broccoli			X	
Cabbage			X	
Carrots			X	
Cauliflower			X	X
Celery			X	
Corn			X	
Cucumbers			X	
Eggplant			X	
Onions			X	
Peppers			X	
Tomatoes			X	
Zucchini		X	X	

Cakes and Dainties

Pretty boxes covered with colorful paper and filled with delicate little cakes or delicious homemade cookies make lovely offerings as gestures of friendship and affection. How many smiles and handshakes are exchanged between friends? Try exchanging gifts from your kitchen—gifts we offer our friends to satisfy the child that lives in all of us!

True—the shelves in our grocery stores display many attractive products, each one possibly more interesting than the one before, and each one a product of another region of the world: butter cookies and wafers from Holland, shortbread from Scotland, and so on. However, nothing can replace the gifts that we have lovingly created with our own hands nor equal the pride with which we offer them.

Preparing such gifts need not take up a great deal of your time. Whether you choose to make our two-tone pinwheel cookies composed of intriguing concentric circles, our delicately flavored rosewater cookies, our spaceship cupcakes or our miniature fantasy cakes to tempt the strongest of wills— any one of these pastries can be prepared in a very short time.

All you need is to choose an occasion: a birthday, an invitation to dinner, a visit to family or friends—or, perhaps, simply to please a loved one.

Two-Tone Pinwheel Cookies

In addition to the contrasting colors, the different patterns that can be created with these cookies incites curiosity. They are attractive to the eye and, of course, the inevitable question is "However did you do that?" The questions fade once the cookies are tasted, however, and "My, but they're delicious!" becomes the predominant remark. Pretty soon the hands stretch out to the plate, decorated with a lacy paper doily, to enjoy a second cookie!

The children should come up with some imaginative theories as to how you made the pinwheels. Let them try to figure it out but keep it your secret. If they guess your secret, next time dazzle them with checkerboard cookies—that should keep them guessing!

Two-Tone Pinwheel Cookies

Level of Difficulty	(utensil symbols)
Preparation Time	20 min
Cost per Serving	$ $
Yield	2 dozen
Cooking Time	1-1/2 min x 4
Standing Time	None
Power Level	50%, 90%
Write Your Cooking Time Here	

Ingredients

125 mL (1/2 cup) butter
125 mL (1/2 cup) sugar
1 egg yolk
375 mL (1-1/2 cups) flour
7 mL (1-1/2 teaspoons) baking powder

2 mL (1/2 teaspoon) salt
60 mL (4 tablespoons) milk
7 mL (1-1/2 teaspoons) vanilla extract
30 g (1 ounce) unsweetened chocolate

Method

— Cream the butter and the sugar; add the egg yolk and continue to beat to a smooth consistency; set aside.
— Sift the flour, baking powder and salt.
— In another bowl, mix the milk and the vanilla.
— Add the dry ingredients, alternating with the milk mixture, to the butter and sugar mixture. Begin and end with the dry ingredients. Mix well.
— Divide the dough into two equal parts and set aside.
— Melt the chocolate at 50% for 30 seconds and blend into one half of the dough.
— Press the two halves of dough flat with your hands and place one on top of the other.
— Roll out the two layers of dough, roll up to form a log and then slice into 24 cookies.
— Place six cookies in a circle on a greased pie plate.
— Place the plate on a raised rack and cook at 90% for 1-1/2 minutes; give the plate a half-turn midway through the cooking.
— Bake the other cookies, six at a time, in the same way.

Cream the butter and the sugar; add the egg yolk and continue to beat to mix well.

Sift the flour, baking powder and salt.

After adding the dry and liquid ingredients to the butter and sugar mixture, divide the dough into two equal parts.

Melt the chocolate for 30 seconds at 50% and blend into one half of the cookie dough.

After pressing the two halves together, roll the dough out and then roll up to form a log; cut into 24 slices.

Bake the cookies, six at a time, on a greased pie plate for 1-1/2 minutes at 90%.

MICROTIPS

Avoid Overbaking Cookies

Most cookies are made of rich dough, the fat in which often causes them to cook too quickly. To avoid overcooking, take them out of the oven as soon as the dough begins to set. Otherwise the center of the cookies will become hard and dry.

Frozen cookies and cookie mixes from supermarkets do not always produce good results when cooked in microwave ovens. The dough does not cook well. Prepare cookies yourself according to recipes in this book to achieve the best results.

Rosewater Cookies

You will find that this cookie recipe pleases your sense of smell as well as your taste buds. The subtle fragrance of roses and sugar that emanates from these cookies produces an aura of calm and sweetness and, thus, with the first bite, the flavor rivals the perfume. Roses and sugar—one does not merely eat these cookies; one savors them and enjoys them, one after another.

22

Rosewater Cookies

Level of Difficulty	🍴🍴
Preparation Time	20 min*
Cost per Serving	$
Yield	approximately 5 dozen
Cooking Time	1-1/2 min x 10
Standing Time	None
Power Level	90%
Write Your Cooking Time Here	

* The dough must be refrigerated for 1 hour before cooking.

Ingredients

250 mL (1 cup) butter
3 eggs
1125 mL (4-1/2 cups) all
purpose flour
375 mL (1-1/2 cups) sugar
45 mL (3 tablespoons) baking
powder

7 mL (1-1/2 teaspoons)
baking soda
5 mL (1 teaspoon) salt
250 mL (1 cup) sour cream
15 mL (1 tablespoon)
rosewater
colored sugar

Method

— Cream the butter and add the eggs, one at a time, beating well after each addition.
— In another bowl, mix all the dry ingredients and add, alternating with the sour cream, to the butter and egg mixture, begin and end with the dry ingredients.
— Add the rosewater and mix well.
— Roll out the dough and then roll up to form a log that is 7 cm (3 inches) in diameter.
— Seal the roll of dough in plastic wrap and refrigerate for 1 hour.
— Cut the roll into thin slices and sprinkle with the colored sugar.
— Place 6 or 7 cookies in a circle on an ungreased pie plate.
— Place the plate on a raised rack and cook at 90% for 1-1/2 minutes. Give the plate a half-turn midway through the cooking.
— Repeat this process until all the cookies are baked.

Assemble all the necessary ingredients for the preparation of these flavorful cookies.

After creaming the butter add the eggs, one at a time, beating well after each additon.

Add the dry ingredients, alternating with the sour cream, to the butter and eggs, begin and end with the dry ingredients.

Roll out the dough and roll into a log that is 7 cm (3 inches) in diameter; cut into thin slices.

Place the cookies in a circle on an ungreased pie plate.

Cook at 90% for 1-1/2 minutes; give the plate a half-turn midway through the cooking.

Chocolate Spaceship Cupcakes

Make your cupcakes into a very special shape—chocolate spaceships! The youngsters will be crazy about them. Little chocolate cupcakes covered with chocolate icing and decorated with candies and icing sugar, they will be a great hit at any birthday party.

These cupcakes will literally take flight from their foil launching pads and will fire up the imaginations of your young, budding astronauts. Imagine the stories that will emerge from the depths of their colorful imaginations, and there'll be no stopping them, except, of course—to take another bite!

Chocolate Spaceship Cupcakes

Level of Difficulty	🍴🍴
Preparation Time	30 min
Cost per Serving	$ $
Yield	1 dozen
Cooking Time	7 min
Standing Time	30 min (in the refrigerator)
Power Level	50%, 70%
Write Your Cooking Time Here	

Ingredients

Cake
2 squares unsweetened chocolate
75 mL (1/3 cup) oil
175 mL (3/4 cup) water
250 mL (1 cup) sugar
1 egg
5 mL (1 teaspoon) vanilla extract
300 mL (1-1/4 cups) flour
2 mL (1/2 teaspoon) salt
5 mL (1 teaspoon) baking soda

Icing
2 squares unsweetened chocolate
50 mL (1/4 cup) butter
325 mL (1-1/3 cups) icing sugar
1 egg
5 mL (1 teaspoon) vanilla extract

Decoration
icing sugar
colored candies

Method

Cake
— Melt the chocolate at 50% for 1 minute and allow to cool.
— Add the oil, water, sugar, egg and vanilla to the cooled chocolate and mix well.
— Sift the flour with the salt and baking soda; gradually add the dry ingredients to the chocolate mixture, beating until smooth.
— Line two muffin pans with No. 75 paper muffin cup liners and fill with the cake batter.

— Place one muffin pan on a raised rack and cook at 70% for 2-1/2 minutes, giving the pan a half-turn midway through the cooking.
— Repeat with the second muffin pan.
— Allow to cool completely before icing.

Icing
— Melt the chocolate at 50% for 1 minute; add the butter, icing sugar, egg and vanilla and beat until smooth.
— Let the icing stand in the refrigerator for 30 minutes.

Decoration
— Cut a slice off the top of each cupcake and set aside.
— Sprinkle the cupcakes with icing sugar.
— Cut each slice that was set aside in half and place the two halves on top of the cupcake so that they are reversed, the cut edges toward the outside.
— Cover the half-slices with icing and decorate with colored candies.

Add the dry ingredients to the chocolate mixture and beat until smooth.

Place one muffin pan on a raised rack and cook six cupcakes at a time at 70% for 2-1/2 minutes.

Give the muffin pan a half-turn midway through the cooking time.

Make the icing by adding the butter, icing sugar, egg and vanilla to the melted chocolate and then beating well.

To make the spaceships, cut a slice off the top of each cupcake and then cut each slice in half.

Decorate the cupcakes by sprinkling them with icing sugar, frosting the half-slices and garnishing with small candies.

MICROTIPS

To Soften Brown Sugar

The microwave oven provides the perfect way to deal with brown sugar that has hardened into a solid block. Simply put the block of sugar into a thick plastic bag and add a little water or a quarter of an apple. Tie a piece of string loosely around the opening. Heat at 100% for 20 seconds and check to see if the sugar has softened. Repeat once or twice as necessary, taking care not to let the sugar melt. When it has softened sufficiently, take it out of the oven and allow it to stand for 5 minutes. If your block of sugar is small (less than 225 g/8 ounces), follow the same procedure but check the sugar every 15 seconds.

Miniature Fantasy Cakes

Individual chocolate cakes, full of flavor, covered with a smooth chocolate sauce and frosted with chocolate icing— three thousand years ago the Aztecs, who used the cocoa bean as a medium of exchange, would have envied such riches. Any lover of chocolate will covet these delicious concoctions. Let your imagination run wild when you decorate these cakes. You might serve them along with the spaceship cupcakes. Now that's an interesting combination!

Miniature Fantasy Cakes

Level of Difficulty	🍴🍴
Preparation Time	15 min
Cost per Serving	$ $
Yield	6
Cooking Time	6 min
Standing Time	None
Power Level	100%, 70%, 30%
Write Your Cooking Time Here	

Ingredients

Cake
10 mL (2 teaspoons) oil
1 egg, well beaten
250 mL (1 cup) sugar
250 mL (1 cup) flour
5 mL (1 teaspoon) baking powder
pinch salt
175 mL (3/4 cup) milk

Chocolate Sauce
125 mL (1/2 cup) butter
50 mL (1/4 cup) cocoa powder
50 mL (1/4 cup) sugar
2 eggs

Chocolate Icing
2 squares chocolate
30 mL (2 tablespoons) butter
325 mL (1-1/3 cups) icing sugar

Method
— First, prepare the cake batter by adding the oil to the well-beaten egg; mix well.
— Add the sugar to this mixture, beating well.
— Sift the flour, baking powder and salt.
— Add the dry ingredients, alternating with the milk, to the egg mixture. Begin and end with the dry ingredients.
— Place the batter in six small glass molds, filling them to the half-way point. Set aside.
— Second, prepare the chocolate sauce by melting the butter at 100% for 1 minute.
— Add the cocoa, sugar and eggs and mix well. Pour the sauce over the cake batter in the molds.
— Place the molds on a raised rack and cook at 100% for 1 minute. Give the molds a half-turn and continue to cook for 2 minutes at 70%.
— Allow to cool completely before unmolding the cakes.
— While the cakes are cooling, prepare the icing by melting the chocolate and butter for 1 to 1-1/2 minutes at 30%.
— Add the icing sugar and beat until smooth.
— Frost the unmolded cakes with the chocolate icing and decorate as desired.

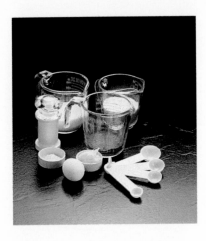

Gather the ingredients needed to prepare these little fantasy cakes.

Make sure the cake batter is well mixed.

Prepare the chocolate sauce by adding the cocoa, sugar and eggs to the melted butter.

Pour the chocolate sauce over the cake batter in each mold.

Remove the cakes from the molds and frost them with the chocolate icing.

Decorate the frosted cakes as desired.

MICROTIPS

Decorating Your Cakes and Dainties

It isn't always necessary to purchase ultra-sophisticated utensils for decorating your cakes and cookies. A simple fork works very well in achieving parallel lines. A fluted cookie cutter creates a pretty scalloped effect on round shapes and fingers dipped in melted chocolate work wonders on filled confections that may be irregular in shape. A pastry bag with a variety of nozzles can be very useful; you can, for instance, fill it with chocolate paler or darker in color than that being used to cover the confection, the contrast will provide a different effect.

Confections

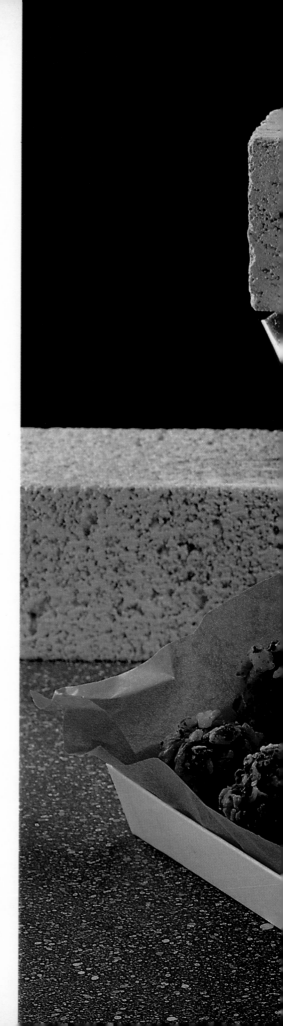

Receiving chocolates or candies and other confections never fails to give pleasure! The delightful ribboned boxes, filled with a variety of fancy sweets, are always touching—and each bite seems unique. The confections you produce in your own kitchen are even more precious to receive because of the time and care you have invested in them. These homemade offerings are a genuine gesture of friendship, the trademark of some well-known confectioner on a box of candy bought in haste paling in comparison.

Confectionery is, by definition, the art of making sweets, including candy. Today, most candy is prepared with white granulated sugar, but other sweetening agents can also be used. Honey, for instance, always a popular ingredient, is often used in the preparation of Oriental confections; in the West, it is also used to flavor confections and to sweeten nougats and caramels. Furthermore, honey is non-crystalline and can be used in recipes for clear candies. Maple sugar and corn syrup are also frequently used by candy makers.

And how can we discuss candy without mentioning chocolate? For many, chocolate is the ultimate confection; for others it is almost a passion. Its unique aroma, its smooth texture and its rich flavor combine to keep one coming back for more. Whether in the form of truffles, wafers or fudge, or used as a frosting, chocolate provides a special magic!

Desert Roses

It was in the fifteenth century, during their explorations of Arab countries, that Western explorers first discovered refined sugar and methods of preserving foods with it. Around the same time, Portuguese merchant ships first carried cargoes of oranges from India to western countries. So precious was this fruit, however, that for a long time its use was restricted to treats on various holidays. But since it was impossible to keep the fruit from spoiling, preserving the oranges became the obvious way of prolonging enjoyment of them.

Today, we are therefore able to use oranges any time to make whatever sugary confection might suit our taste, such as our extraordinary recipe for desert roses: candied oranges, chocolate, vanilla, sugar and almonds—a delightful treat worthy of your very best friends!

Desert Roses

Level of Difficulty	🍴🍴
Preparation Time	20 min
Cost per Serving	$ $
Yield	1 dozen
Cooking Time	23 min
Standing Time	None
Power Level	100%, 70%, 90%, 50%
Write Your Cooking Time Here	

Ingredients

50 mL (1/4 cup) butter
250 mL (1 cup) sugar
7 mL (1-1/2 teaspoons) vanilla extract
250 mL (1 cup) 35% cream
300 mL (1-1/4 cups) slivered almonds
175 mL (3/4 cup) candied oranges, diced
2 to 3 squares sweetened dark chocolate

Method

— In a microwave-safe bowl mix the butter, sugar and vanilla.
— Cook the mixture at 100% for 5 minutes or until it is lightly browned; mix several times so that the mixture is uniform in color.
— Add the cream and cook at 70% for 3 minutes or until the sugar has melted. Mix every minute during the cooking time.
— Add the almonds and the candied oranges; mix well.
— Cook at 70% for 10 minutes or until mixture thickens; mix well 2 or 3 times during the cooking.
— Divide the batter into 12 portions, pouring into 2 microwave-safe muffin pans; cook one pan at a time, on a raised rack, at 90% for 1 to 1-1/2 minutes.
— Allow the desert roses to cool completely before removing from the pans. Set aside.
— Melt the chocolate at 50% for 1 to 2 minutes.
— Cover the desert roses with the melted chocolate.

Mix the butter, sugar and vanilla in a microwave-safe bowl.

Stir the mixture several times during the cooking period so that it is uniform in color.

Add the cream and continue to cook, stirring every minute.

Add the almonds and the candied oranges; mix well.

Pour the batter into the muffin pans.

Allow to cool and cover the desert roses with the melted chocolate.

MICROTIPS

Avoid Overcooking

Certain foods continue to cook even at the end of the microwave cooking time. For this reason, a standing time is usually included in the cooking cycle. A potato may appear to be slightly firm when it comes out of the oven but the heat continues to disperse itself uniformly inside the vegetable while it is standing. It is therefore important to adhere to the standing times indicated in microwave recipes. This time will vary according to the food. Remember that the standing time is the final step in any recipe and has as much significance as all the steps prior to it.

Nut Fudge

Fudge is a fondant type of candy that is especially popular here in our country. This recipe for fudge is derived from the traditional European fondant but enriched with evaporated milk or cream. Like its predecessor, fudge is basically a sugar-based syrup cooked to the soft ball stage (see the chart on page 13). It can be flavored with coffee, chocolate, vanilla or honey and the texture can be varied by adding almonds or other nuts, whole, chopped or slivered. If you prefer firm, granular fudge, beat the syrup while it is hot; if you want soft, creamy fudge, wait until the syrup is lukewarm before beating—the syrup will then thicken and crystallize into a smooth, uniform fudge.

Nut Fudge

Level of Difficulty	🍴🍴
Preparation Time	10 min
Cost per Serving	$ $
Yield	2 dozen squares
Cooking Time	12 min
Standing Time	2 hours (in the refrigerator)
Power Level	100%
Write Your Cooking Time Here	

Ingredients

300 mL (1-1/4 cups) fine granulated sugar
2 mL (1/2 teaspoon) baking powder
175 mL (3/4 cup) evaporated milk
120 mL (6 tablespoons) butter
5 mL (1 teaspoon) vanilla extract

225 g (8 ounces) milk chocolate chips
60 g (2 ounces) walnuts, coarsely chopped
60 g (2 ounces) pecans, coarsely chopped
60 g (2 ounces) almonds, coarsely chopped

Method

— Put the sugar, baking powder, evaporated milk and butter into a microwave-safe bowl and mix well. Cook at 100% for 11 to 12 minutes, stirring every 2 minutes.
— Test the cooking stage by dropping a little of the mixture into cold water; it should form a soft ball.
— Add the vanilla extract to the mixture and beat with an electric hand mixer at high speed for 2 minutes.
— Add the chocolate chips and continue to beat until they have melted.
— Add the walnuts, pecans and almonds and mix well.
— Pour the mixture into a greased pan and let stand in the refrigerator for at least 2 hours.
— Cut the fudge into small squares before serving.

In a microwave-safe bowl mix the sugar, baking powder, evaporated milk and butter; cook at 100% for 11 to 12 minutes.

Stir every 2 minutes during the cooking period.

Test the cooking stage by dropping a bit of the mixture into cold water; it should form a soft ball.

Add the vanilla extract and beat with an electric hand mixer at high speed for 2 minutes.

Add the chocolate chips and continue to beat until they have melted.

Add the walnuts, pecans and almonds to the mixture before pouring into a greased pan.

Orange Wafers

A chocolate-covered graham wafer base, garnished with a blend of icing sugar, milk and orange extract—such is the composition of our orange wafers. The eyes of your friends will light up at the sight of this confection. Once they have tasted your wafers the silence of complete satisfaction and contentment will be followed by exclamations of delight, not to mention requests for a second helping. Just make sure you have plenty on hand because they will disappear rapidly, and soon your gift box will be empty!

Level of Difficulty	¶¶¶
Preparation Time	15 min
Cost per Serving	$ $
Yield	1 dozen
Cooking Time	3 min
Standing Time	1 hour (in the refrigerator)
Power Level	50%, 100%
Write Your Cooking Time Here	

Ingredients

12 graham wafers
175 g (6 ounces) chocolate chips
45 mL (3 tablespoons) butter
250 mL (1 cup) icing sugar

2 mL (1/2 teaspoon) orange extract
4 drops orange food coloring
30 mL (2 tablespoons) milk

Method

— Spray a 20 cm (8 inch) square pan with a non-stick spray.
— Line the bottom of the pan with the graham wafers. Set aside.
— Melt the chocolate chips and 15 mL (1 tablespoon) of the butter at 50% for 2 minutes; stir once during the cooking.
— Pour the chocolate over the wafers. Spread the chocolate evenly with a spatula and let stand in the refrigerator for 1 hour.
— Melt the remaining butter at 100% for 30 seconds and add the icing sugar, the orange extract and the food coloring.
— Add just enough milk to make the mixture smooth and uniform.
— Using a spatula, spread this mixture evenly over the surface of the cold chocolate.
— Store in the refrigerator.

MICROTIPS

Adapting Traditional Cake Recipes

Ingredients:
1. When adapting a recipe for the microwave never reduce the quantity of eggs as you would the water or oil.
2. The quantity of sugar can be reduced without unbalancing the chemical composition of the cake. Of course, reducing the amount of sugar depends on your taste or diet and not on the fact that you are using a microwave oven.

3. If you wish to use whole wheat flour instead of white flour remember that whole wheat flour is heavier: 400 mL (1-2/3 cups) of this flour equals 500 mL (2 cups) white flour.
4. Cake recipes for the microwave generally require more baking

Gather all the ingredients needed to prepare these delicious orange wafers.

Pour the melted chocolate into a square pan lined with graham wafers.

Spread the chocolate evenly over the crackers and then refrigerate for 1 hour.

Add the icing sugar, orange extract, food coloring and the milk to the remaining melted butter.

Pour the orange mixture over the cold chocolate.

Spread the orange mixture evenly over the chocolate and store in the refrigerator. Cut into squares before serving.

powder. However, first try adapting a traditional recipe using the same quantity. If the results are not satisfactory, try reducing the amount of liquid. Increase the amount of baking powder only as a last resort.

Method:
1. Since the time required for microwave cooking is shorter than traditional oven cooking the batter and dough have less time to rise. When adapting a traditional recipe, let the dough stand 5 to 10 minutes before cooking so that the yeast has time to react.
2. Never flour a pan before microwave cooking. Use crumbled graham wafers or breadcrumbs. Better yet, spray the inside of the pan with an anti-stick coating.

White Chocolate Truffles

Truffles are made of a mixture of chocolate, butter and cream, whipped together to produce a fluffy confection that will win every candy lover's heart. They are shaped into small balls, about the size of walnuts. The name "truffle" derives from the mushroom of the same name; although a totally different food, its richness and its popularity constitute the similarity.

To obtain a round shape, refrigerate the mixture before shaping the candy, then coat each one with cocoa powder, icing sugar or finely chopped almonds. Pack the truffles in a box covered with brightly colored paper and lined with a lacy paper doily. The effect will be fantastic! Don't store them for too long as they are at their best for only the first forty-eight hours.

White Chocolate Truffles

Level of Difficulty	
Preparation Time	10 min
Cost per Serving	$ $
Yield	2 dozen
Cooking Time	3 min
Standing Time	20 min (in the refrigerator)
Power Level	50%
Write Your Cooking Time Here	

Ingredients
115 g (4 ounces) white chocolate
50 mL (1/4 cup) 35% cream
1 egg yolk
15 mL (1 tablespoon) butter

10 mL (2 teaspoons) white rum
375 mL (1-1/2 cups) icing sugar
almonds, finely chopped

Method
— Melt the chocolate at 50% for 2 to 3 minutes; stir midway through the cooking.
— Whip the cream and add to the melted chocolate.
— Add the egg yolk and the butter; mix well.
— Add the rum.
— Sift the icing sugar and add to the mixture, beating to a smooth consistency.
— Let the mixture stand in the refrigerator for 20 minutes or until it becomes very firm.
— Divide the mixture into 24 portions, and form these into small balls. Roll in the chopped almonds.
— Store the truffles in the refrigerator for no more than 2 days.

Nut Truffles

Ingredients
90 g (3 ounces) butter
200 g (7 ounces) dark chocolate
90 g (3 ounces) icing sugar
5 mL (1 teaspoon) vanilla extract
90 g (3 ounces) chopped nuts

Method
— Melt the butter and the chocolate at 50% for 2 minutes, stirring halfway through the cooking.
— Add the icing sugar and vanilla extract; mix well.
— Add 60 g (2 ounces) of the chopped nuts to the mixture; set the remaining nuts aside for coating the truffles.

— Refrigerate the mixture for 30 minutes.
— Shape the mixture into small balls and roll them in the chopped nuts.
— Wrap the truffles individually in plastic wrap.
— Store in the refrigerator for no more than 2 days.

Melt the chocolate at 50% for 1 to 1-1/2 minutes; stir once and resume the cooking at the same power level for another 1 to 1-1/2 minutes.

Add the whipped cream to the melted chocolate.

Add the egg yolk and the butter to the chocolate and cream mixture; mix well.

Sift the icing sugar and add to the mixture, beating well to obtain a smooth consistency.

Divide the refrigerated mixture into 24 portions and shape into small balls.

Roll each truffle in the finely chopped nuts.

Apricot Almond Swirls

Although the apricot was discovered in the region of Beijing (Peking) and the Romans, as well, were familiar with this fruit, it was not until the seventeenth century that the apricot was fully appreciated. Today, it enjoys a choice reputation in gourmet cooking as well as in the day-to-day cooking with which we are concerned.

The flavors of chocolate, almond paste and walnuts, together with the flavor characteristic of the apricot, combine to make our apricot almond swirls a treat for the palate. It is with great pride that you will offer these delicacies to your friends and neighbors.

Apricot Almond Swirls

Level of Difficulty	🍴🍴
Preparation Time	30 min*
Cost per Serving	$ $ $
Yield	2 dozen
Cooking Time	2 min
Standing Time	None
Power Level	100%, 50%
Write Your Cooking Time Here	

* The apricots should steep in apricot liqueur for 2 hours.

Ingredients

125 mL (1/2 cup) dried apricots, finely chopped
50 mL (1/4 cup) apricot liqueur
200 g (7 ounces) almond paste

125 mL (1/2 cup) icing sugar
115 g (4 ounces) sweet chocolate
24 walnuts

Method

— Place the apricots in a microwave-safe bowl and add the apricot liqueur. Cook at 100% for 45 to 60 seconds and allow the apricots to steep in the liqueur for 2 hours.
— Add the almond paste to the apricots and beat with an electric hand mixer.
— Add the icing sugar, mix well and knead the apricot dough.
— Shape the dough into a roll 30 cm (12 inches) long and 2.5 cm (1 inch) in diameter.
— Cut the roll into 24 rounds, 1.25 cm (1/2 inch) thick, and place them in the refrigerator.
— Melt the chocolate at 50% for 1 minute or until it is just melted.
— Using a fork, dip each round of dough into the melted chocolate.
— Allow the excess chocolate to drain and place the swirl on a piece of waxed paper.
— Garnish each swirl with a walnut.

Place the chopped apricot and the apricot liqueur in a microwave-safe bowl; cook at 100% for 45 to 60 seconds.

Beat together the almond paste and the steeped apricots with an electric hand mixer.

Add the icing sugar and then knead the apricot dough.

Shape the dough into a roll 30 cm (12 inches) long and 2.5 cm (1 inch) in diameter; slice into 24 rounds, 1.25 cm (1/2 inch) thick.

Using a fork, dip each round into the melted chocolate.

Garnish each apricot almond swirl with a walnut.

MICROTIPS

To Make Cakes Rise Properly

Cake batter must be very thoroughly mixed, not only to blend the ingredients well but also to ensure the even distribution of the tiny air bubbles that cause the cake to rise. We also recommend that you let the batter stand for 5 minutes before putting it into the microwave oven, thus allowing the leavening agent to begin to work. Otherwise, the cake may not rise properly in the center.

Coconut Squares

No one knows for certain where coconut was originally discovered but many seem to think it was first found in India. One fact is certain, however, coconut was known and appreciated by the native peoples of the Americas long before the arrival of the European conquerors.

In cooking, coconut is often combined with the aromatic essence of vanilla and when you add the rich flavor of brown sugar—you have a confection to rave about! This combination, in our recipe for coconut squares, will result in a taste treat that will be greatly appreciated by everyone.

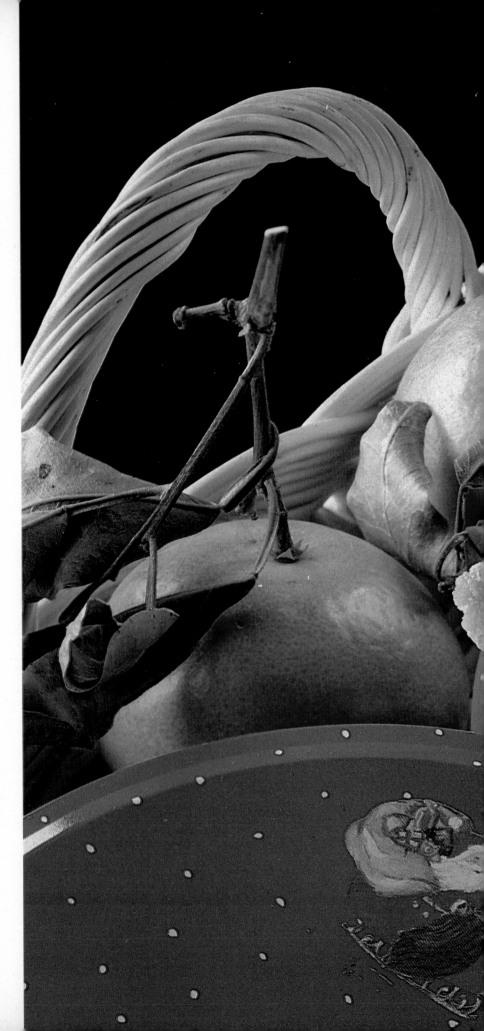

Coconut Squares

Level of Difficulty	
Preparation Time	20 min
Cost per Serving	$
Yield	1 dozen
Cooking Time	15 min
Standing Time	None
Power Level	100%, 50%
Write Your Cooking Time Here	

Ingredients

50 mL (1/4 cup) butter
300 mL (1-1/4 cups) brown sugar
250 mL (1 cup) flour
2 eggs
5 mL (1 teaspoon) vanilla extract

5 mL (1 teaspoon) baking powder
150 g (5 ounces) dried coconut

Method

— Melt the butter at 100% for 45 seconds; stir and add 50 mL (1/4 cup) of the brown sugar.
— Add the flour and mix well.
— Press this mixture into a 20 cm (8 inch) square dish.
— Place the dish on a raised rack and cook at 50% for 4 to 6 minutes or until the center is cooked; give the dish a half-turn midway through the cooking.
— Allow to cool.
— Put the remaining brown sugar, the eggs, vanilla, baking powder and 90 g (3 ounces) of the coconut in a bowl; beat with an electric hand mixer until thoroughly mixed.
— Spread this mixture over the cooked flour and sugar base.
— Place the dish on a raised rack and cook at 50% for 6 to 8 minutes or until the center is cooked; give the dish a half-turn midway through the cooking.
— Garnish with the remaining coconut and allow to cool.
— Cut into squares before serving.

Gather all the ingredients needed for the preparation of these delicious coconut squares.

Melt the butter; add 50 mL (1/4 cup) of the brown sugar and the flour and mix well.

Press the mixture into a square cake pan that can be used in the microwave.

Place the dish on a raised rack and cook the mixture at 50% for 4 to 6 minutes; give the dish a half-turn halfway through the cooking time.

Spread the mixture of the remaining brown sugar, the eggs, vanilla, baking powder and coconut over the cooked flour and sugar base.

Cook at 50% for 6 to 8 minutes or until the center is cooked; give the dish a half-turn midway through the cooking.

Date Delights

Dates are the fruit of a palm tree known as the date palm and are harvested in certain regions of Africa in the month of October. Dates were known in ancient times and formed a staple in the diet of nomadic desert tribes. It is said that Mohammed himself was partial to the flavor of the date.

Today, dates are traditionally used in baking but not often used in making candy. In our recipe for date delights, we break this tradition; the delicious flavor of dates combines with a sugar syrup to produce a delicious confection. Surprise your friends with this unique gift—they will be delighted!

Date Delights

Level of Difficulty	
Preparation Time	10 min
Cost per Serving	$ $
Yield	2 dozen
Cooking Time	9 min
Standing Time	20 min
Power Level	100%, 70%
Write Your Cooking Time Here	

Ingredients

150 g (5 ounces) pitted dates, chopped
125 mL (1/2 cup) fine granulated sugar
45 mL (3 tablespoons) butter
50 mL (1/4 cup) milk
1 egg

2 mL (1/2 teaspoon) vanilla extract
60 mL (4 tablespoons) corn flakes, crushed
60 g (2 ounces) walnuts, chopped
60 g (2 ounces) coconut

Method

— In a microwave-safe bowl mix the dates, sugar and butter.
— Cook the mixture at 100% for 3 minutes, stirring midway through the cooking.
— Beat with a wooden spoon until very well mixed.
— In another bowl combine the milk, egg and vanilla and mix well.
— Add a small amount of the hot date mixture to the milk mixture and then gradually add the milk mixture to the date mixture, beating constantly.
— Cook at 70% for 5 to 6 minutes or until the mixture thickens; stirring twice during the cooking.
— Allow the mixture to cool by letting it stand for 15 to 20 minutes.
— Divide the mixture into 24 portions and shape into small balls.
— Mix the corn flakes, walnuts and coconut and roll each date ball in this mixture.
— Store in the refrigerator.

In a microwave-safe bowl mix the dates, sugar and butter.

Cook the mixture at 100% for 1-1/2 minutes; stir and cook at 100% for another 1-1/2 minutes.

Gradually add the milk mixture to the date mixture, beating constantly.

Cook the date mixture at 70% for 5 to 6 minutes or until it thickens, stirring twice during the cooking.

Divide the mixture into 24 portions and shape into small balls.

Mix the crushed corn flakes, the chopped walnuts and the coconut and roll each date ball in this mixture.

MICROTIPS

Fresh Homegrown Herbs

Herbs have an incomparable flavor, especially when very fresh. A number of herbs can be cultivated in flower pots, like house plants. Dill, basil, chives, coriander, marjoram, parsley, rosemary, savory, sage and thyme all need sunlight. Bay leaves and verbena, on the other hand, grow best in the shade. Chervil, lemon balm, tarragon and mint adapt to either sunlight or shade.

Caramel Crunch

Sugar and corn syrup for a golden caramel, peanuts and peanut butter for rich flavor as well as crunch, and raisins just for fun—add all these to a graham wafer base and you have an original recipe that will create a tradition among your friends.

Of course, they will want the recipe. It's up to you—you may share it or, better still, keep it your secret. The mystery will make your gift even more precious. One thing is certain; everyone will enjoy them!

Caramel Crunch

Level of Difficulty	🍴
Preparation Time	10 min
Cost per Serving	$ $
Yield	1 dozen squares
Cooking Time	9 min
Standing Time	20 min
Power Level	100%, 90%
Write Your Cooking Time Here	

Ingredients

12 graham wafers
125 mL (1/2 cup) sugar
500 mL (2 cups) corn syrup
175 g (6 ounces) roasted

unsalted peanuts
225 g (8 ounces) crunchy peanut butter
115 g (4 ounces) raisins

Method

— Line a 20 cm (8 inch) square microwave-safe pan with the graham wafers; set aside.
— Put the sugar and the corn syrup into a microwave-safe bowl and mix well.
— Cook the mixture at 100% for 4 to 6 minutes or until it just reaches the boiling point, stirring twice during the cooking. Continue to cook at 90% for another 3 minutes.
— Add the remaining ingredients to the hot syrup and mix well.
— Pour the mixture over the wafers and let stand for 15 to 20 minutes.
— Cut the caramel crunch into 12 squares and wrap individually.

MICROTIPS

How to Determine the Amount of Pectin in Fruit

Here is a quick, simple trick for determining the amount of pectin in a particular fruit. You may find this useful in deciding how much pectin to add when preserving fruit. Place 5 mL (1 teaspoon) of the juice of the fruit you wish to use in a cup with 30 mL (2 tablespoons) of methyl hydrate and stir. Wait 1 to 2 minutes until the fruit juice begins to thicken. A few gelatinous particles at the bottom of the cup indicate a low level of pectin, while a large amount of gelatin, making the juice quite thick, indicates a high level of pectin. Once you have done this test, make sure that the mixture is discarded and the cup is thoroughly washed, as methyl hydrate is highly toxic.

Place the graham wafers in the bottom of a square pan.

In a microwave-safe bowl mix the sugar and the corn syrup and cook at 100% for 4 to 6 minutes.

Stir the syrup twice during the cooking and continue to cook at 90% for 3 minutes.

Add the peanuts, peanut butter and raisins to the syrup; mix well.

Pour the syrup mixture over the crackers and let stand for 15 to 20 minutes.

Cut the caramel crunch into 12 squares and wrap individually.

Chocolate-Covered Bananas

Our recipe for chocolate-covered bananas represents pure tradition in the art of the confectioner: coating fresh fruit with melted chocolate!

For the best results you must add oil to the chocolate, then melt until the chocolate is completely fluid and wait until it cools slightly before dipping the fruit. If the chocolate is too hot, it will drip off the fruit without coating it; if it is too cool, whitish streaks will appear on its surface. To keep the melted chocolate at the proper temperature, place the bowl of chocolate in a container filled with hot water. You will thus be able to dip the chunks of banana at your own speed.

Decorated with a combination of chocolate and bright, colorful sprinkles, these dainty confections are festive, fun and delicious!

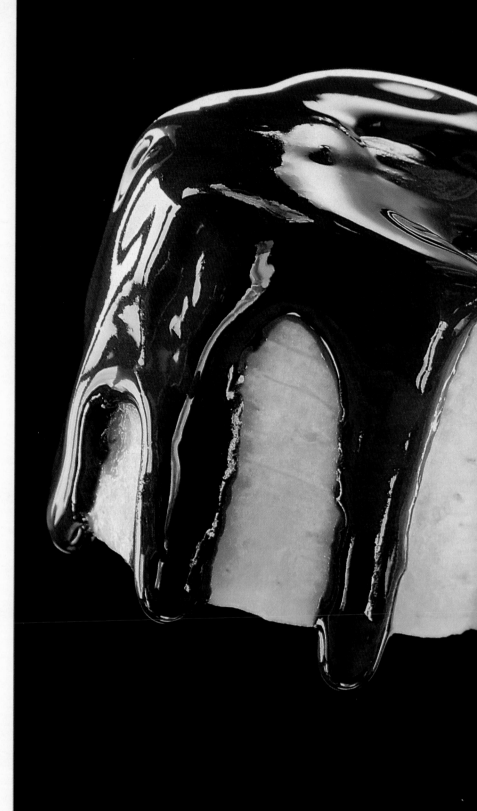

Chocolate-Covered Bananas

Level of Difficulty	▯▯ ▯▯
Preparation Time	20 min
Cost per Serving	$
Yield	approximately 3-1/2 dozen pieces
Cooking Time	5 min
Standing Time	15 min
Power Level	50%
Write Your Cooking Time Here	

Ingredients

5 bananas, very firm
340 g (12 ounces) chocolate chips
30 mL (2 tablespoons) oil

chocolate cake-decorating sprinkles
colored cake-decorating sprinkles

Method

— Cut the bananas into 2.5 cm (1 inch) long pieces.
— In a microwave-safe bowl, mix the chocolate chips and the oil and cook at 50% for 3 to 5 minutes, or until the chocolate is just melted, stirring twice during the cooking.
— Stick a toothpick into each piece of banana.
— Dip each piece into the melted chocolate.
— Combine the chocolate and colored cake-decorating sprinkles in a bowl and coat the chocolate-covered banana pieces with them.
— Let stand, allowing to cool, for 10 to 15 minutes.

MICROTIPS

Making Candied Flower Petals

The petals of roses, violets, rose geraniums and freesia are edible; candied, they add a lovely decorative touch to all kinds of confectionery.

In a bowl, mix one part powdered gum arabic (a natural product found in specialty shops) with two parts rosewater. With a soft paint brush carefully cover each petal, or the entire flower, with this mixture. Arrange on a plate, sprinkle with sugar and allow to dry near a heat source until they become very firm in texture and are easily crumbled.

Slice the bananas into 2.5 cm (1 inch) long pieces.

Add the oil to the chocolate chips and melt at 50% for 3 to 5 minutes, stirring twice during the cooking.

Stick a toothpick into each piece of banana.

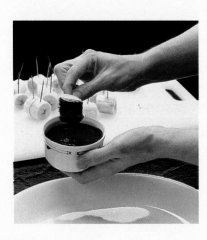

Dip the chunks of banana into the melted chocolate, coating them partially.

Coat the chocolate-covered portion of each banana chunk with a mixture of chocolate and colored cake-decorating sprinkles.

Let the banana pieces stand for 10 to 15 minutes and store in the refrigerator until you wish to serve them.

MICROTIPS

To Measure Fat Ingredients Easily

Pour 125 mL (1/2 cup) cold water into a measuring cup and drop the butter, lard or shortening by spoonfuls into the cup until the level of the water reaches the desired quantity of the fat ingredient plus 125 mL (1/2 cup).

Peanut Brittle

Peanut brittle lovers—rejoice!
This recipe is so easy that it
is ideal for a first attempt at
candy making: success is
assured. You need only cook
the corn syrup and sugar to
the caramel stage (see the
chart on page 13) and then
add the peanuts. Vanilla is
your flavoring agent. Stir the
mixture and pour into pans;
use a greased spatula to
spread the caramel in the
pans and allow it to cool.
Break the peanut brittle into
pieces, wrap in colored
plastic wrap and tie with a
perky bow. A delicious gift—
and so simple to prepare!

Peanut Brittle

Level of Difficulty	🍴
Preparation Time	10 min
Cost per Serving	$ $
Cooking Time	13 min
Standing Time	None
Power Level	100%
Write Your Cooking Time Here	

Ingredients

450 g (1 lb) extra fine granulated sugar
300 mL (1-1/4 cups) corn syrup
1 mL (1/4 teaspoon) salt
340 (12 ounces) salted peanuts

30 mL (2 tablespoons) butter
7 mL (1-1/2 teaspoons) vanilla extract
5 mL (1 teaspoon) baking powder

Method

— Place the sugar, corn syrup and salt in a microwave-safe bowl; mix well and cook at 100% for 9 to 11 minutes, stirring twice during the cooking.
— Add the peanuts to the syrup and mix well.
— Cook at 100% for 1 minute; stir and continue cooking at 100% for another minute.
— Add the butter, vanilla and baking powder and mix vigorously until the mixture is smooth and creamy.
— Pour the mixture on a greased cookie sheet and spread evenly with a greased spatula.
— Allow the peanut brittle to cool.
— Break the candy into pieces and wrap in individual portions.

MICROTIPS

Do Not Overbeat Cake Batter

The ingredients which make up a cake batter are in a fragile chemical balance. For this reason, avoid overbeating the batter as this prevents the cake from rising.

Cooking with Sugar

If your mixture contains a lot of sugar, for example a syrup, take care not to cook it for longer than the recipe directs. Sugar can get hot very quickly, at which point it may burn.

Place the sugar, corn syrup and salt in a microwave-safe bowl and mix well.

Cook the mixture at 100% for 9 to 11 minutes, stirring twice during the cooking.

Add the peanuts to the syrup and mix well.

Continue to cook at 100% for 2 minutes, stirring midway through the cooking.

Add the butter, vanilla and baking powder and stir vigorously.

Pour the peanut brittle on a greased cookie sheet and spread evenly.

Peanut Butter Cups

What delight you will experience when you offer these delicious confections to your friends. Molded chocolate cups—filled with creamy peanut butter, graham wafer crumbs and icing sugar—then topped with more melted chocolate. What a treat!

Served with strong coffee or your favorite tea, these peanut butter cups cannot be equalled. For variety, try replacing the filling with fondant and cherries or with . a favorite fruit jelly. The possible variations on this wonderful recipe are endless. You are limited only by your imagination!

Peanut Butter Cups

Level of Difficulty	🍴🍴🍴
Preparation Time	30 min
Cost per Serving	$ $
Yield	2 dozen
Cooking Time	6 min
Standing Time	30 min
Power Level	50%
Write Your Cooking Time Here	

Ingredients
30 mL (2 tablespoons) butter
50 mL (1/4 cup) smooth
peanut butter
75 mL (1/3 cup) graham
wafer crumbs
50 mL (1/4 cup) icing sugar
225 g (8 ounces) chocolate
chips

24 paper candy cups

Method
— Put the butter and peanut butter into a microwave-safe bowl and mix.
— Cook the mixture at 50% for 3 minutes, stirring twice during the cooking.
— Gradually add the graham wafer crumbs and the icing sugar to the hot peanut butter; mix well and set aside.
— In another microwave-safe bowl melt the chocolate chips at 50% for 2 minutes, stirring halfway through the cooking.
— Upon removing from the oven, place the bowl of melted chocolate in a container of hot water.
— Pour 5 mL (1 teaspoon) of the melted chocolate into each paper cup, tipping it to coat the sides. Make sure that the bottom and fluted sides are completely coated; let stand for 15 to 20 minutes to cool. Set the remaining chocolate aside.
— Place a small spoonful of the peanut butter mixture in each chocolate cup.
— Re-melt the remaining chocolate at 50% for 30 to 60 seconds.
— Pour the melted chocolate into the molds, making sure it covers the peanut butter filling.
— Let stand in the refrigerator for at least 10 minutes.
— Wait until the chocolate is completely cool before removing the paper.

Mix the butter and peanut butter in a microwave-safe bowl; cook at 50% for 3 minutes, stirring twice during the cooking.

Gradually add the graham wafer crumbs and the icing sugar to the hot peanut butter mixture; set aside.

To prevent the melted chocolate from cooling too quickly, place the bowl containing the chocolate in a container of hot water.

Pour 5 mL (1 teaspoon) of the melted chocolate into each paper cup. Make sure the fluted sides are well coated with chocolate.

Place a small spoonful of the peanut butter mixture in each chocolate cup.

Fill the cups with the remaining melted chocolate. Refrigerate, allow to cool completely before removing the paper cup.

MICROTIPS

Molded Chocolate Cups—A Unique Decorative Touch!

Here is a simple but fun way to use tiny molded chocolate cups without the peanut butter filling. Float a chocolate cup, filled with cream, in a cup of coffee or hot cocoa. It will float for a few seconds before melting, the chocolate and cream then gently spreading throughout your hot drink. This dainty decoration will surprise everyone, not to mention the flavor it will add. Serve your beverages immediately though, as the chocolate cups melt very quickly.

Sponge Toffee

Level of Difficulty	🍴🍴
Preparation Time	10 min
Cost per Serving	**$**
Cooking Time	15 min
Standing Time	None
Power Level	100%
Write Your Cooking Time Here	

Ingredients

250 mL (1 cup) sugar
375 mL (1-1/2 cups) corn syrup

15 mL (1 tablespoon) vinegar
15 mL (1 tablespoon) baking soda

Method

— In a large microwave-safe container mix the sugar, corn syrup and vinegar.
— Cook the mixture at 100% for 11 to 13 minutes, stirring twice during the cooking.
— Test the syrup by dropping a very small spoonful into a glass of cold water. A few balls should form. If the balls are a little sticky, the syrup is ready. If not, continue to cook at 100% for another 1 to 2 minutes.
— Quickly add the baking soda to the syrup, mix well and pour into a greased square pan.
— Allow the toffee to sit at room temperature until it becomes hard.
— Cut the toffee into small pieces and wrap them in individual portions.

MICROTIPS

Checkerboard Cookies

The two-tone pinwheel cookies (see recipe, page 20) can be transformed into cookies with other impressive patterns, such as a checkerboard pattern. Roll out the two portions of cookie dough (the pale and the dark) with a rolling pin. Paint one portion with beaten egg white and lay the other portion on top. Roll again to make sure both strips stick together and even off the edges of the rectangle thus formed. Divide this rectangle lengthwise into three equal parts, paint each with beaten egg white and place one on top of the other. The rectangle thus obtained presents three alternating bands of color. Sprinkle the rolling pin with icing sugar and roll lightly over the rectangle of dough to make sure each strip sticks to the next. Divide the rectangle into four equal parts, lengthwise, and place on top of each other, alternating the colors to produce the effect of a checkerboard. Finally, cut into slices and bake.

Candied Fruit Peel

The preservation of fruits in sugar is a time-honored technique. Plums, cherries, the flesh of pineapple and peaches and the peel of citrus fruits have always been candied with great success. This procedure has continued to this day because the fruit and peel thus prepared are unequalled. They have a firm texture and a delightful aroma. The recipe for candied fruit peel that we present is a classic; however, the use of the microwave is a recent innovation. You will find the results you obtain delightful.

Serve the candied fruit peel in very hot coffee or tea to enjoy the flavor at its best. It also makes an effective garnish for ice cream—and all sorts of other desserts as well.

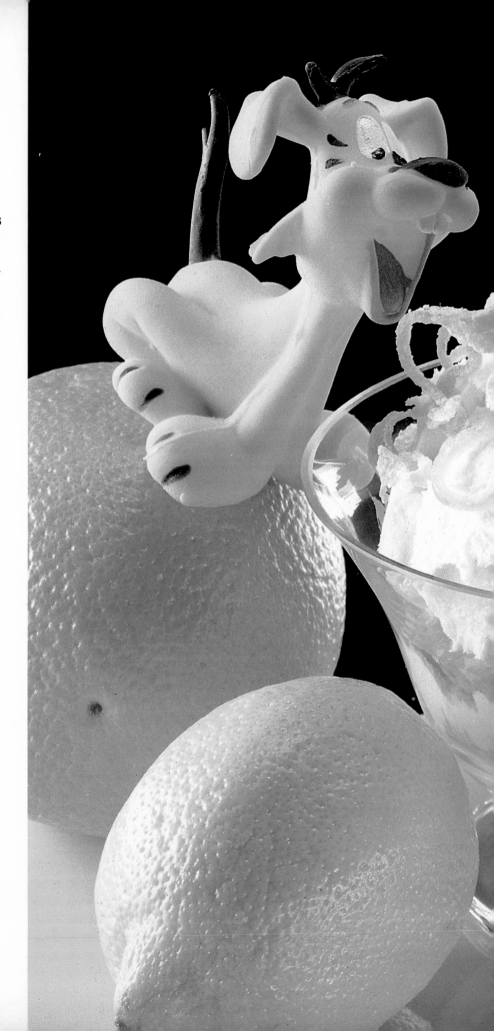

Candied Fruit Peel

Level of Difficulty	(3 utensils)
Preparation Time	30 min
Cost per Serving	$
Cooking Time	22 min
Standing Time	None
Power Level	100%
Write Your Cooking Time Here	

Ingredients
1 lemon
1 orange
1325 mL (5-1/2 cups) water
150 mL (2/3 cup) sugar
icing sugar to taste

Method
— With a paring knife, peel the fruit. Cut the peel into thin strips and set aside.
— Pour 50 mL (1/4 cup) of the water into a microwave-safe bowl; add the sugar and cook at 100% for 30 seconds. Stir and set aside.
— Pour 425 mL (1-3/4 cups) of the water into a microwave-safe bowl. Add the strips of peel, and cook at 100% for 5 minutes and drain.
— Cook the peel again in the same way two more times, using fresh water and draining each time.
— Rinse the peel and sponge it carefully with paper towel.
— Add the peel to the syrup and cook uncovered at 100% for 6 minutes. Stir midway through the cooking.
— Drain the peel with a strainer and place on a rack. Allow to partially cool.
— Sprinkle both sides of the peel with icing sugar and allow to cool completely.
— Store the candied fruit peel in covered jars.
— Serve in coffee, hot chocolate fondue or with ice cream. Candied fruit peel can also be used as a garnish for many other desserts.

With a paring knife remove the peel from the fruit, cut into thin strips and set aside.

Prepare the syrup by adding the sugar to 50 mL (1/4 cup) of the water; cook at 100% for 30 seconds.

Cook the strips of peel for 5 minutes, using 425 mL (1-3/4 cups) of fresh water. Repeat these steps 3 times.

Rinse the peel and carefully sponge with paper towel.

Place the peel in the syrup and cook uncovered at 100% for 6 minutes.

Place the drained peel on a rack and allow to partially cool. Sprinkle both sides of the peel with icing sugar and allow to cool completely before storing in jars.

Preserves

"And I will come, bearing gifts of preserves," wrote the author Victor Hugo. In the nineteenth century gifts of preserves were highly appreciated. Even today, nothing equals the pleasure of offering the best and freshest of the season's produce, preserved with great care.

Of course, it is now possible to obtain seasonal products all year round, imported or grown in hothouses, but the flavor does not equal that of freshly grown produce in season. The different methods of preserving allow us to enjoy our produce picked at the height of the season and preserved at its best.

Whether you wish to preserve in order to keep all the natural qualities of your produce just as they are or to change the flavor and the texture by combining different ingredients, preserves allow you to capture the best of the seasons. You may choose to preserve fruit and vegetables as they are by using sugar, salt, vinegar or alcohol, or you can make them into jams, jellies, pickles, relishes and other condiments. But not every preserving agent lends itself to any fruit or vegetable. A glance at the chart on page 15 will help you determine which agent is appropriate for the food you wish to preserve.

Preserves have become a symbol of the past times. They evoke another era, another way of life: a time of kitchen gardens; of fruit ripening on the vines and gathered only at the height of its flavor; of personal cookbooks in which one recorded treasured homemade recipes; of hand-printed labels and preserve cupboards, with children climbing on chairs to reach tempting jars of preserves at any price. How delightful to recapture such simple joys as the making of preserves and offering them as very personal gifts.

Zucchini Jam

The original recipe for a jam with marrow appeared for the first time in *Le Ménagier de Paris* during 1393. Not only did this recipe constitute a simple method of preserving but it was a precious condiment that was served with pride. The recipe we offer you consists of zucchini cooked in water to which has been added sugar, lemon juice, pineapple and apricot jelly powder. Delicious!

However, both zucchini and pineapple contain very little pectin; therefore, if you like your jam quite firm, simply add a few more drops of lemon juice.

Level of Difficulty	🍴
Preparation Time	20 min
Cost per Serving	$
Yield	1 L (4 cups)
Cooking Time	11 min
Standing Time	None
Power Level	100%
Write Your Cooking Time Here	

Ingredients

1.5 L (6 cups) zucchini, grated
1 L (4 cups) sugar
juice of half a lemon

250 mL (1 cup) pineapple, crushed
1 170 g (6 ounces) package apricot jelly powder

Method

— Put the zucchini in a microwave-safe bowl; cover and cook at 100% for 4 to 6 minutes or until the zucchini is completely cooked.
— Add the sugar, lemon juice and pineapple; continue to cook at 100% for 4 to 5 minutes, stirring twice during the cooking.
— Add the apricot jelly powder and mix thoroughly. Allow to cool before placing in sterilized jars.
— Store the zucchini jam in the refrigerator.

MICROTIPS

How to Prepare Coconut

Packaged, grated or shredded coconut can always be found in a supermarket. However, when fresh coconuts are available for use in desserts, the results cannot be compared.

Start by cutting through the fibrous tuft on the peaked end of the coconut; then with a metal skewer pierce the three eyes found there and turn the coconut on to its open end, allowing the milk to drain. Crack the outer shell by giving it several sharp raps at about one-third of its length with a mallet or the back edge of a cleaver. Remove the white pulp, which separates quite easily from the outer shell. Before grating cut it into pieces and remove the brown skin that covers the pulp.

For Successful Mousses

Certain fresh fruit, such as pineapple, contain enzymes that prevent gelatin from setting. To make a successful pineapple mousse you must cook the fruit first, which destroys the enzymes, or use canned fruit rather than fresh.

Also, several alcoholic beverages can be used to give other mousses a delicious flavor. Madeira, for example, adds character to the taste of apricot and a coffee liqueur emphasizes the rich taste of mocha. Sweet white wine, kirsch, maraschino and even champagne can also be used as flavoring agents.

Assemble all the ingredients needed to prepare this delicious recipe.

In a covered container cook the grated zucchini at 100% for 4 to 6 minutes.

Add the sugar, lemon juice and pineapple and continue to cook at 100% for 4 to 5 minutes.

Stir the mixture twice during the cooking.

Add the apricot jelly powder and mix well. Allow to cool.

Allow the zucchini jam to cool before placing in jars. Store in the refrigerator.

MICROTIPS

Choosing Vegetables for Blanching

Blanching remains the best way to prepare vegetables for long-term storage, whether you intend to freeze or to preserve them. However, you must choose the vegetables you wish to store with great care. They should be very fresh, of choice quality and as young and tender as possible. Whatever method you choose will only preserve the vegetables as they are; it will not improve them.

Cranberry Preserve

What a pleasure it is to have a dish of homemade cranberry preserve on the table as a condiment to accompany the traditional turkey on festive occasions. Cranberries, oranges, sugar and candied ginger blend their flavors to tempt the palate. Its subtle aroma, its wonderful texture and its rich, mellow taste evoke thoughts of spicy chutneys. But why wait for holidays to offer it? This cranberry condiment will enhance any poultry dish, winter or summer.

Cranberry Preserve

Level of Difficulty	🍴
Preparation Time	15 min
Cost per Serving	$ $
Yield	1 L (4 cups)
Cooking Time	10 min
Standing Time	None
Power Level	100%
Write Your Cooking Time Here	

Ingredients

2 oranges
675 g (1-1/2 lbs) cranberries
175 mL (3/4 cup) sugar

60 g (2 ounces) candied ginger

Method

— Remove the orange zest with a vegetable peeler and squeeze the oranges to extract the juice. Cut the zest into fine strips.
— Put the cranberries, the juice and zest of the oranges, the sugar and candied ginger into a microwave-safe bowl and mix well.
— Cook at 100% for 8 to 10 minutes or until the mixture is juicy, stirring twice during the cooking.
— Spoon the mixture into sterilized jars and allow to cool.
— Store the cranberry preserves in the refrigerator.

MICROTIPS

Making Your Jams, Jellies and Marmalades Set Properly

A proper balance between the pectin, the sugar and the acidity in fruit is necessary to obtain a successful jam or jelly. The seeds, the flesh and the skin of most fruit contain pectin, a substance that is soluble as well as gelatinous. Heated with the sugar and acid in a given fruit, the pectin thickens and allows jams, jellies and marmalades to set. Fruit that is rich in pectin is usually very acidic; cooked with sugar, it produces a marmalade that is very firm. Fruit that is less acidic has less pectin; to succeed with such fruit you must add other fruit that is rich in pectin, lemon juice or commercial pectin. The first solution usually produces very good results. Here is a chart that will no doubt inspire some interesting combinations.

Fruit High in Pectin (medium or high acidity)	Fruit Medium in Pectin (medium or low acidity)	Fruit Low in Pectin (medium or low acidity)
lemons, currants, grapefruit, limes, apples, plums, oranges	apricots, blueberries, raspberries, mandarins, grapes	pineapple, nectarines, cherries, figs, strawberries, passion fruit, melons, peaches, pears, rhubarb

Assemble all the ingredients needed to prepare this delicious preserve.

With a vegetable peeler remove the zest from the oranges; cut the zest into fine strips.

Put all the ingredients in a large microwave-safe glass bowl; mix well and cook at 100% for 8 to 10 minutes.

Stir the mixture twice during the cooking.

Spoon the cranberry mixture into preserving jars.

Allow to cool and then store in the refrigerator.

95

Apple Chutney

By definition, chutney is a mixture of fruit or vegetables preserved in vinegar, sugar and spices. It is the perfect condiment to accompany any meat dish. In this recipe, a long cooking time allows for the tender flesh of the apples to combine with the flavors of onion, garlic, raisins, sugar and spices. This is one of the simplest and most economical ways of preserving fruit with vinegar. Contrary to most other preserves, in making chutneys you can make use of older, bruised foods—you need only remove the spoiled parts. This apple chutney is bound to take you back to the preserves of your childhood!

Apple Chutney

Level of Difficulty	🍴🍴
Preparation Time	30 min
Cost per Serving	$
Yield	500 mL (2 cups)
Cooking Time	25 min
Standing Time	None
Power Level	100%
Write Your Cooking Time Here	

Ingredients

675 g (1-1/2 lb) cooking apples
1 onion, finely chopped
1 clove garlic, crushed
50 mL (1/4 cup) raisins
10 mL (2 teaspoons) fine herbs

2 mL (1/2 teaspoon) sage
5 mL (1 teaspoon) salt
375 mL (1-1/2 cups) apple juice
45 mL (3 tablespoons) vinegar
50 mL (1/4 cup) sugar

Method
— Peel the apples, remove the cores and cut into quarters.
— Put all the ingredients into a large microwave-safe bowl; mix well and cook at 100% for 20 to 25 minutes, stirring every 5 minutes.
— Make sure the apples are well cooked at this point; if they are not, continue to cook until they are very soft.
— Spoon the hot chutney into sterilized preserving jars and allow to cool.
— Store the chutney in the refrigerator.

MICROTIPS

To Preserve the Zest of Oranges and Lemons

If you have grated too much orange or lemon zest, or if you simply wish to prepare some in advance, it can be stored for several days. Simply place the zest in a sealed container and store in the refrigerator.

To Prevent a Compote from Becoming a Purée

When one prepares a compote of mixed fruit, one risks obtaining either a purée or a fruit mixture in which some fruit is overcooked and other fruit undercooked. Such disappointing results can be avoided by adding the different fruits at different times,

Assemble all the ingredients necessary to prepare this delicious apple chutney.

Carefully peel the apples and remove the cores.

Cut the apples into quarters.

Put all the ingredients into a large microwave-safe bowl and mix well.

Cook the chutney at 100% for 20 to 25 minutes, stirring every 5 minutes.

Spoon the apple chutney into preserving jars and allow to cool before refrigerating.

depending on how much time each takes to cook.

Large, firm fruit such as apples, pears and peaches should be cooked first. To speed up the cooking time, cut them into halves or quarters. Chunks of fresh pineapple and rhubarb should be added at the beginning as well. Interrupt the cooking to add fruit of medium firmness, such as oranges, cherries, bananas and grapes. Finally, just before the end of the cooking period, add the more fragile fruit: melons, mulberries and raspberries. Following this method and with a little practice, a perfect compote of beautiful fruit—cooked so that they melt in the mouth—can be prepared.

Marinated Antipasto

Unlike chutney, which is a mixture of well-cooked fruit and vegetables, pickles are generally pieces of fruit or vegetables gently cooked and then marinated in vinegar. This procedure preserves all the natural characteristics of the food. Flavors are varied by the addition of alcohol or different vinegars such as malt, wine or cider vinegar; spices are added for seasoning and also to help in the preserving process. The recipe that follows, a classic from the Italian school of cooking, makes a delightful antipasto. These pickles, served as an appetizer with a terrine of veal, will greatly enhance its delicate flavor. Delicious!

Marinated Antipasto

Level of Difficulty	🍴🍴
Preparation Time	30 min
Cost per Serving	$ $
Yield	approximately 2 L (8 cups)
Cooking Time	12 min
Standing Time	2 to 3 days
Power Level	100%
Write Your Cooking Time Here	

Ingredients

3 carrots
1 green pepper
1 red pepper
125 mL (1/2 cup) Brussels sprouts
125 mL (1/2 cup) small whole mushrooms
125 mL (1/2 cup) cauliflower flowerets
125 mL (1/2 cup) broccoli flowerets
125 mL (1/2 cup) water
14 black olives

Marinade
300 mL (1-1/4 cups) water
140 mL (5/8 cup) cider vinegar
15 mL (1 tablespoon) salt
15 mL (1 tablespoon) oil
1 clove garlic
1 bay leaf
pinch basil
pinch oregano

Method

— Prepare the vegetables: cut the carrots into sticks 2.5 cm (1 inch) long and slice the peppers into strips of the same length; set aside. Clean the Brussels sprouts and brush the mushrooms.
— In a covered container cook the Brussels sprouts, the cauliflower and broccoli in the water at 100% for 5 to 6 minutes; stir halfway through the cooking time.
— Drain the vegetables and dry with paper towel. Allow to cool.
— Prepare the marinade: put the water, vinegar, salt and oil in a large measuring cup and mix well; cook at 100% for 4 to 6 minutes or until the mixture reaches the boiling point.
— Add the garlic, bay leaf, basil and oregano; stir and set aside.
— Place all the vegetables and the olives in a large sterilized wide-mouthed jar.
— Fill the jar with the marinade and let stand in the refrigerator for 2 to 3 days before serving. The marinated antipasto should be stored in the refrigerator.

Prepare all the vegetables as described in the method.

Prepare the marinade by cooking the water, vinegar, salt and oil. Then add the garlic, bay leaf and spices. Set aside.

In a covered container, cook the Brussels sprouts, cauliflower and broccoli in water at 100% for 5 to 6 minutes. Drain.

Dry the vegetables with paper towel and allow to cool.

Place the vegetables and olives in a large wide-mouthed jar.

Fill the jar with the marinade and let stand in the refrigerator 2 to 3 days before serving. The marinated antipasto should be stored in the refrigerator.

Microwave Confectionery: Practical Tips

Success in baking pastry, as in making candy, often depends on details which, if overlooked, can transform a promising recipe into a dismal failure. Here, then, are a few practical tips that you may find useful.

Cooking

— Never flour pans for use in the microwave. Use crumbs, crushed graham wafers or even breadcrumbs. An even better method is to coat the pans with a non-stick substance such as Pam.

— Do not extend the cooking time for pastry or candy containing sugar beyond that which is indicated in the recipe as sugar attracts the microwaves; the internal temperature of the food will rise rapidly and it will burn.

— Always use dishes that are heat-resistant to thicken syrups or to melt sugar, otherwise, they too will burn.

— For success in baking or candy making it is important to work in a cool, dry room; excess heat and humidity can, in some cases, spoil certain recipes that have a cooked sugar base.

Utensils

— The flavor of certain fruits, especially those high in acid, changes upon contact with metal. Therefore, it is best to use strainers with nylon rather than metal mesh to strain syrups made from these fruits.

— Before rushing out to buy new equipment to use in your microwave oven, check your cupboards; any non-metallic pan or dish can be used in the microwave.

— Use round dishes or tube pans whenever possible. Microwave energy is distributed in such a way that food in the corners of square or rectangular dishes tends to cook more quickly than food in the center.

Ingredients

— Grating chocolate is difficult because it tends to stick to the grater and melt in your fingers. You can avoid these problems by refrigerating both the chocolate and the grater before grating.

— The recipes in this volume call for large eggs. If large eggs are not available, calculate the amount of egg needed by basing your calculation on 1 large egg being equivalent to 50 mL (1/4 cup).

— If cookies baked in the microwave are not as brown as you wish, substitute dark brown sugar for white sugar; if you use brown sugar, however, extend the cooking time for a few seconds. Also, you can have darker cookies by using whole wheat flour instead of white, all purpose flour.

Confectionery Terminology

Anti-crystallizing agent:
A substance which, when added to sugar syrup, prevents the formation of crystals as the syrup cools. It is used mainly in the production of suckers and clear hard candies.

Bain-marie:
Smaller containers of food are placed in a vessel containing boiling water and the food can be gently cooked, melted, reheated or kept warm.

Blanching:
To plunge fruit or vegetables into boiling water and then to cool rapidly in cold water in order to peel more easily, to reduce acidity or to partially cook before freezing or preserving.

Candied:
The result of a procedure used to preserve fruit and vegetables that consists of soaking them in a sugary liquid and then allowing them to dry out.

Crystallization:
The solidification of a sugar syrup. Crystallization can be partial or complete, depending on the desired texture.

Garnish:
The art of cutting various fruit, vegetables and other foods into decorative shapes to enhance the appearance of food.

Génoise:
A light cake, originating in Genoa, Italy. The batter is different from other cake batters in that the eggs are not separated and are kept warm in a *bain-marie* while being beaten. This cake is the basis for many light and delicate cake-based desserts as well as for filled cakes of all kinds.

Paraffin: A solid white waxy substance used for making candles, for making waxed paper and for sealing jars containing preserves.

Piping nozzle: A small cone-shaped tip that attaches to a cloth or paper pastry bag and is used to decorate cakes and other confections. Different shapes of nozzles permit a variety of decorations for desserts.

Preserve: A food or a combination of foods that has been placed or cooked in a solution (sugar, vinegar, salt or alcohol) and then sealed in airtight containers in order to preserve it.

Reduce: The action of boiling a liquid in order to reduce its volume, thereby enhancing its flavor and producing a thicker texture.

Scum: A froth that forms on the surface of jam during cooking.

Simmer: To cook over a gentle heat without allowing the mixture to come to a full boil.

Sweetener: A sweet substance (honey, syrup, sugar) used to sweeten liquids and mixtures that are bitter as well as to neutralize preparations that are too acidic.

Zester: A utensil used to peel thin strips of orange or lemon zest in such a way as to separate the exterior, colored, flavored peel from the bitter white membrane that covers the fruit.

Culinary Terms

Apples *à la dauphine*: Peeled apples with the cores removed, baked in the oven and then allowed to cool. They are served on a bed of Condé rice and covered with an apricot syrup flavored with kirsch.

Apricot turnovers: Apricot halves, peeled, sprinkled with sugar and then wrapped in a layer of puff pastry that has been coated with egg yolk. They are baked in the oven and sprinkled with icing sugar before serving.

Chantilly cream: Whipped cream flavored with vanilla.

***Condé* rice:** Rice cooked in sweet milk and flavored with vanilla.

***Dragée*:** Almond or praline covered in a hard sugar coating.

Mincemeat: A pie or tart filling made with suet, sugar, spices and dried fruits. Mincemeat is a traditional English preserve; cognac is used as the preserving agent.

Nougat: A confection made with caramelized sugar or honey combined with almonds, walnuts or hazelnuts.

Piccalilli: A condiment composed of an assortment of vegetables cooked and preserved in a mustard sauce.

Truffle: A light, fluffy candy made with semi-sweet chocolate. It is shaped into a small ball about the size of a walnut. It takes its name from a mushroom that is very rare and extremely rich. Both foods are considered exotic.

Conversion Chart

**Conversion Chart for the
Main Measures Used in
Cooking**

Volume		Weight	
1 teaspoon	5 mL	2.2 lb	1 kg (1000 g)
1 tablespoon	15 mL	1.1 lb	500 g
		0.5 lb	225 g
1 quart (4 cups)	1 litre	0.25 lb	115 g
1 pint (2 cups)	500 mL		
1/2 cup	125 mL		
1/4 cup	50 mL	1 oz	30 g

**Metric Equivalents
for Cooking
Temperatures**

49°C	120°F	120°C	250°F
54°C	130°F	135°C	275°F
60°C	140°F	150°C	300°F
66°C	150°F	160°C	325°F
71°C	160°F	180°C	350°F
77°C	170°F	190°C	375°F
82°C	180°F	200°C	400°F
93°C	200°F	220°C	425°F
107°C	225°F	230°C	450°F

Readers will note that, in the recipes, we give 250 mL as the
equivalent for 1 cup and 450 g as the equivalent for 1 lb and
that fractions of these measurements are even less
mathematically accurate. The reason for this is that
mathematically accurate conversions are just not practical in
cooking. Your kitchen scales are simply not accurate enough to
weight 454 g—the true equivalent of 1 lb—and it would be a
waste of time to try. The conversions given in this series,
therefore, necessarily represent approximate equivalents, but
they will still give excellent results in the kitchen. No problems
should be encountered if you adhere to either metric or
imperial measurements throughout a recipe.

Index